TAKE THREE

Soundswrite Press New Poets

Volume 1

SwP
SOUNDSWRITE
PRESS

First published in 2019 by
SOUNDSWRITE PRESS
52 Holmfield Road
Leicester LE2 1SA

www.soundswritepress.co.uk

ISBN: 978-0-9954578-1-2

Copyright of poems resides with authors as listed

Cover background image: Polygonal Texture available from
www.dribbble.com/Lumberjacks

Typeset in Gills Sans MT & Cambria
Front cover font IM Fell French Canon
Fell Types are digitally reproduced by
Igino Marini www.iginomarini.com

Printed and bound by Imprint Digital

Acknowledgements:

The editors would like to thank Samantha Aylward for help with desk top publishing and cover design. Tuesday Shannon would like to thank her family and friends, as well as her colleagues and supervisors at Nottingham Trent University for their continued support. Pippa Hennessy would like to thank Writing East Midlands for awarding her a place on their mentoring scheme, and in particular Sarah Hymas, her mentor.

Thanks are due to the editors of the following magazines and anthologies where some of the poems or earlier versions first appeared: Tuesday Shannon – *Bystander anthology (Launderette Books, 2017)*; Pippa Hennessy – *Antiphon, Brittle Star, Ink Sweat & Tears, The Interpreter's House;* Elizabeth Hourston – *Lines Review, Literary Review, Soundswrite Press poetry anthologies (2011, 2015).*

TAKE THREE

TUESDAY SHANNON	5
PIPPA HENNESSY	33
ELIZABETH HOURSTON	65

TUESDAY SHANNON

Contents

Passing through	7
Precipitation	8
Desdemona	9
Oz	10
Satis House	11
Greenock Cemetery	12
Number 6	13
Wallpaper flowers	14
Pisces	15
Pit Lane	16
Vandalism	17
Leaving Chesterfield	18
Barcelona	19
Dedication	20
Long distance	21
Memory foam	22
Exhumation	23
Scala	24
Souvenirs	25
Halogen streetlights	26
Regulars	27

Passing through

Summer nights here smell of kebab shops and petrol;
some boy racer revs his clapped-out Corsa
as streetlights flicker in the evening dim.
Payday has filled pubs
that have sat near empty all month,
each one seeping music from open windows.
Heavy doors swing wide
and out floods a flock of girls in too-high heels
stumbling, negotiating cracks in the cobbles.
Their bus pulls up close to the kerb, shudders to a stop
and they pause, turn, check themselves
in half-reflections on tinted glass;
then, with the squeal of rubber on tarmac,
it's as though they were never there.

Precipitation

Even the locals can feel it build
as the temperature rises a degree a day,
the air gets so thick sweat beads trickle
down bronzed legs from the backs of knees,
dampen the plump white cushioning of trainers.

Three whole weeks
tempers shorten by the minute

when the sky finally gives way
boys dance outside the bar,
shirts off, faces tilted up;
girls laugh, bent over, clutching
stomachs; droplets race down bare shoulders,
soaking the thin white cotton of summer dresses.

Desdemona

We are stripped
of agency by men
who fail
to see: love
is not conquest
but treaty.

Oz
After The Wizard of Oz

She lies across her bed,
the weight of another
cowardly scarecrow
with a clockwork heart
pushing her into the pillows
pushing into her;
hands pull through hair,
and with every motion,
bare heels knock together.

Follow the Yellow Brick Road.

Yellow. Yell. Oh. Yes.
Monochrome gives way
to Technicolor.
He rolls away   not far enough.

She pulls the blanket tighter;
still not back in Kansas.

Satis House
After Great Expectations

My hand was stopped
halfway to the altar, so pause
the ticking of the clocks, keep
their hands forever apart.

Let the dust settle, they said. It's settling, still
on the wedding breakfast – money wasted.
And if the shoe were on the other foot?
I never would have deceived him.

Bring me a daughter,
name her for the stars.
I'll give her room to grow,
pour ice into her heart.

In these rooms, do not move a thing;
I shall wear this dress until
its lace becomes a second skin.
In this house, I will die twice.

Greenock Cemetery

After every wedding, christening and funeral
we visit the grandparents who left before I arrived –

there, my mother sees her own ghost –
aged nine with her brothers, out
for a picnic with their mother – freckled faces
furrowed with confusion, because Grandma would never appear.

At the graveside, she turns to me:

When I die, don't bury me here.

I thought you'd like to come home.

She smiles. *No. You'll never visit. Besides,*
her hand grips mine,
home is where my children are.

Number 6

Mum would throw a blanket between
washing lines, improvise a hammock
and we would lie: her, me and my sister,
laughing in the afternoon breeze,
my feet dangling over the edge
in silver glitter jelly shoes
that squeezed and gave
my chubby toes blisters.
I refused to give them up.

The doorway was laddered with lines
where Mum would drag a pen over our heads
as proof that here, we flourished.

The garden gate creaked under my weight,
but still I would swing on it,
waiting for visits from a father
who never came, until I stopped waiting
and only the wind would worry its hinges.

Wallpaper flowers

Eyes scan the twists
of hibiscus and heather;
already sure of the next turn,
traced by smaller hands,

fingers, sticky with jam,
left behind smeared outlines
of the routes taken:

strawberry stains, that soap
didn't lift.

Pisces

Conch shell
siphons the sound of the sea.

Pressed to my ear
waves call me back;

the rush of my blood
resonating in the cavity

the shore
so close

that to lick lips
is to taste salt.

Pit Lane

...the land/caves in on the lowest worked-out seam.
Tony Harrison, 'v.'

My grandad's first job was down the pit;
mine was in the theme park built on top of it.
The pit-wheel was joined by a log flume slide,
made in '87, the highest drop on a water ride.

We'd visit each summer when I was a kid,
and ride The Missile until we were giddy or sick.
And Auntie Betty would argue about legal tender:
It's frae Scotland, naw fuckin' America.

We'd take a picnic, the food was overpriced,
and find a good spot if the weather stayed nice,
with legs stretched out so boot-cut jeans could dry
after getting soaked for the sixth, the seventh time.

And no one thought about what it used to be –
like Callaghan and Wilson, Thatcher was history,
just a name that made Uncle Pete scowl and sneer:
she's the reason there's fuck all around here.

But it was sinking into the looted hollow
and shut down for good a decade ago.
The bits that worked were shipped out, sold off
and, once again, Pit Lane leads to rubble and dust.

Vandalism

On the redbrick canvas
of crumbling factory walls
you wrote your name in black marker,
next to tags and phone numbers
promising 'a good time'.

On the teenage cusp of everything,
we knew nothing of permanency,
we were only sure that we would leave
this place behind and that our futures
must be brighter than grey skies
and subsiding mines.

We didn't know that these factories
would become open-plan flats with solid
wood floors, charging rent that the locals
could never afford.

Today the windows are being replaced:
double-glazed sash, overlaid muntins
giving an illusion of divided
light; that wall, bulldozed to rubble. I sift
through it, searching
for the brick that bears your name.

Leaving Chesterfield

Slate grey sky, smudged
like partially erased pencil
clutters with graphite shaded clouds:
threatens to throw sweet
wet drops onto cold ground.

Delayed. Expected 17:27

The station shop bustles
with dishevelled commuters
paying over the odds for Pepsi Max
and packets of Walkers.

Platform 2

A couple cuddle under
the picket fence canopy
as clouds capsize, concrete
reverberates under
worn-out soles.

Coach C

Cheek to glass, droplets
cast freckle shadows on
slickened skin.

Barcelona

Gracias por no fumar
I light a cigarette
before boarding the train
to Sants. Catalan countryside
becomes suburbs behind the film screen
of the window then
the darkness of the Metro.
Green Line Three
where I contort myself
between an armpit and a bony elbow.
La proxima estación es... Liceu.
Emerging into bright daylight;
there she is, as she was:
La Rambla.
Bienvenido a Barcelona.
The pavement glistens with the memory of rain.
Straight ahead is the port where ships
stand to attention in the shadow of Nelson.
Quiero una sangria y una paella por favor, señor.
Your favourite restaurant's
not there anymore. It's another keepsake cavern
filled with fridge magnets, fabric fans,
the tourists you always hated
in their socks, flip-flops and factor fifty.
¡Viva España!
This city is still yours.
Perdona señorita, dónde está Paral-lel?
My feet take the right turn,
past the Bureau de Cambio
and *¡Sabates! ¡Rebaixes! ¡Rebaixes!*
in the Zapateria window.
There, unnoticed by most, between
the pharmacy and the supermarket,
the glass panelled door to our old apartment:
Bienvenido a Casa.

Dedication

The air conditioning stuttered
its dying gasp in the middle of July.
The nights were hardly cooler
than the midday heat
and when we couldn't sleep
despite fans, no sheets,
we pulled the mattress
from its frame, out of the sliding doors
onto the cool ceramic tile
of the balcony. When we woke, my leg
and shoulder were burned to a hot
red stain. You were in the shade.

Long distance

Their silence is half-companionable,
he pretends to read the same line
fourteen times;
she glances over
whenever the road allows.

What?

Nothing.

The wipers swish away,
as they resume the lie
that it was less
than something
that turned her head.

Memory foam

The mattress was replaced
after the remains
of an imagined future departed
her, soaking the foam,
staining the cotton.

The new one didn't squeal
when she shifted in sleep,
but the stillness
like the unopened boxes
in the bathroom cabinet,
and the neatly pressed clothes
in the drawers of the other room,
only served as a reminder:
once, her body was his hearse.

Exhumation
After Seamus Heaney

Coaxed, timidly, from the ground,
where they lie in wait:
dig them out.
Brush away extraneous debris
revealing bleached white bones,
fissures and breaks exposed,
to be re-articulated at the joint
or laid out for viewing: syntax, stanza and line
spaced along the backbone.

Scala

Cigarette smoke twists
lazily, lit by the projector's glare.
Before the interval she strides
down the aisle carrying treats
and a tin rattling loose change,
ready for the rush of sweethearts
from double seats.

Now, there's no intermission
and the new owners ripped out
the double seats, replaced
plush red velvet with
blue polyester

but the smell of decades old
tobacco still filters through licks
of paint and from worn-down carpet,
and the view from the top of the walkway
is unchanged:

silhouettes, sweethearts,
the projector's glare.

Souvenirs

Faded Polaroids and Mardi Gras beads,
pebbles and seashells from some distant beach,
expired tickets and old magazines,
slogan t-shirts and ripped-up jeans

we are the things stored in attic boxes:
broken, half-forgotten, tangled
in fairy lights and unravelled string.

Halogen streetlights

1

deaden
on row after row after row
of parked cars.

The town is silent
until the squeal of a fox foraging
in an upturned wheelie bin
and the bell of the church peals
off a single chime.

2

pierce the black weight
of sky. Headlights bob
and flicker, moving together.

Damp breath fogs the air
and beneath us, grass sweats
morning dew

we will be gone
before blackbirds
break the stillness
and the sun begins its climb.

Regulars
To everyone at The Warren

1

Friday, payday, pub grub and a pint;
he drinks away the dissatisfaction,
tells the barmaid she's pretty and stumbles home,
kebab in hand.

Saturday night:
Jager, Sambuca, Tequila:
anything exotic to stop thoughts
of the week ahead.

Spends Sunday taking the kids he hardly sees
but pays for anyway, to visit his mother
who doesn't even remember their names. Or his,
in a care home that smells of stale piss
and sponge puddings, knowing it all starts again

Monday and the only thing that gets him
through is the thought of

Friday, payday, pub grub and a pint.

2

Every Thursday
she brings company
and revels in the delight
of conversation
that's not been bought;
to be asked about her
grandchildren, now at university,
and the salsa lessons
she takes on Monday nights.

Other mornings her watery latte
goes cold as bar staff clear tables,
pour pints, and her half-started
conversations are abandoned
at the demand of another customer.

3

His fist is as soft as a block
of butter, shaking
around two pound coins
and a twenty pence piece,
to be exchanged
for the first pint of the day.

Under the tap it pours
itself, clouds, settles:
thick and brown with
a white halo the width
of forefinger and thumb.

His skin is the jaundiced shade
of pages in antique books,
and the ink of a decades-old tattoo
is blurred beyond comprehension

not that it matters
whether it reads *Mother*
or *Martha*, those who meant enough
to be honoured are long gone

nothing left but this
small pleasure: the glass
sweats as the tremors still.

4

Maggie says the soup kitchen
kicked her out for shouting
at this guy who's just served
twenty years of a life sentence –
drags her index finger
across her throat.

Says she's used to defending herself:
she knows what *'folk round 'ere'*
think of her.

She takes a £10 note from her
parka pocket, places it on the bar,
tallow film sticks and drags
in pools of dried lager.

What's it coming to when you can't even get a bowl of fucking soup?

PIPPA HENNESSY

Contents

The standard model of particle physics	34
$\sigma_x \sigma_p \geq \frac{\hbar}{2}$	36
$\|v'_x - v_x\| \Delta p_x \approx \frac{\hbar}{\Delta t}$	38
Heisenberg's dawn	40
Simply put, mass bends light	41
Antimatter	42
Quantum dating	44
Blackboard	45
A proton as a serving of minestrone	46
Waltz	48
Rebirth as a quantum mechanic	50
Counting virtual particles	52
Randomness	54
White dwarf (a day by the sea)	56
The strong interaction	58
Collisions	59
Decay	60
Jubilate Astra et Hominem	61
Glossary	62

The standard model of particle physics

The standard model of particle physics contains four fundamental forces.
    The strong nuclear force
        explains how we stay whole.
    The weak nuclear force
        dictates the outcome of our decay.
    Gravitational force
        attracts us to each other.
    Electromagnetic force
        pushes us apart.

The standard model does not explain
    the force of gravity
        why I can't stop my hand
        falling on my wife's grey hair.

The standard model does not explain
    the expansion of the universe
        how we are all separating
        at an increasing rate.

The standard model does not contain
    dark matter particles
        what else would have pulled
        the light from my father's eyes?

The standard model contains
    three generations of quarks and leptons
        but no unborn child
        though I know mine briefly lived.

The standard model does not explain
    the emptiness of my son's bedroom
        or the way the lawn grows
        now he's not here to mow.

The standard model does not explain
> how my other child has changed
>> or how she remains the same white-haired boy
>> who always arrives late.

The standard model does not reflect
> the photograph albums on my shelves
>> there are no equations for stories
>> calculated by images.

The standard model imagines
> three colours and three anti-colours
>> but not the greying of my hair
>> and my need to dye it regularly.

The standard model ignores
> a crying baby's needs
>> and the inconstant value of time
>> in my wife's arms.

$$\sigma_x \sigma_p \geq \frac{\hbar}{2}$$

When your son becomes a woman
(who still fancies women)
in a relationship with a gay man,

when she rejects the name
you carefully picked out
before he was born,

then her father grieves
for the son he's lost,
struggles to love his daughter.

When you don't know how
to talk about him (her?)
when she was a boy,

when you have to think
before everything you say,
have I got the pronouns right?

When she steps out in a skirt
rocking her purple heels
clutching a black purse,

then you feel her distress
as she bathes, bubbles
masking her body's mistakes.

Then your stepmother asks,
do you think it's a phase?
and you can't know it isn't.

When the same eyes
smile from the same face,
the same lips speak the same words,

then you realise she is your child –
here, moving forwards,
the unreduced constant.

Note:

The title is Kennard's derivation of Heisenberg's **uncertainty principle** which states that for two complementary variables, such as position and momentum, the more precisely one is known, the less precisely the other can be known.

$$|v'_x - v_x|\Delta p_x \approx \frac{\hbar}{\Delta t}$$

I saw my daughter yesterday,
tangled hair red from her shoulders
to the base of her spine, blonde-rooted.
When she was a boy, it was white.

I delivered him late, with long nails.
I slipped when cutting them, licked
the speck of blood. My tears
sprinkled his fuzzed head.

Slow to start, I saw her grow
as fast as I could measure his height
stopping only when she needed
to bend to kiss my forehead.

For her fourth birthday, she asked us
for a Barbie doll. His dad and I
laughed, said *don't believe
everything adverts sell you.*

Boys' playground games were alien
to her, standing alone at the edge.
She didn't like colouring,
teachers told him *it's a treat*

for the good boys and girls.
They didn't know she's colour blind,
didn't care. *Not all children like
colouring*, I told him. *It's OK.*

When Spider-Man fought
for his life, she wept on my lap,
anxious about the tears
in his new finely-sewn costume.

I see my daughter now, peeking
from behind my son's eyes.
I see my daughter, and I don't know
what equation describes her.

Note:

The title is Bohr's formulation of the **observer effect**, that simply observing a phenomenon necessarily changes that phenomenon.

Heisenberg's dawn

each subatomic particle of the sun
has a precise probability of being
in any location in the universe
even on the tip of Einstein's tongue

it is only when the sun rises
and the probability functions collapse
that Heisenberg can say to his wife
the sun will shine in the sky today

Simply put, mass bends light

It was a day for apple picking,
unburdening old branches.

Sun-spotted, cool and firm,
each apple kissing lightly as it moved

from branch to hand to basket
branch to hand to basket

branch to hand to basket...
until twilight swallowed the lustre

and, drunk like wasps
on fermented windfalls,

we bedded them in glistening rows
along slat-gaps of new cellar shelves,

stalks downwards, dimpled bottoms
exposed. Picked out bruised ones

for chutney, shut out the light.
Took turns stirring the copper pan

by the flickering oil lamp. *Oh look*,
you murmur, collapsing the silence.

I think I've always known
mass bends light. How else

could sun-spatters startle
from a copper pan of apple chutney?

Antimatter
...excited antihydrogen atoms are expected to glow the same colour as regular hydrogen... (Wikipedia)

At home, I decohere.
My elements become entangled
with the environment,

                      In the lab, you play
                      with the stuff
                      that makes us all,

mother + wife + provider +
comforter + peacemaker
= lost. I am anti-me,

                      joining pre-made particles:
                      antiproton + positron
                      = antihydrogen,

a woman turned
inside out by reaching
for what is beyond reach,

                      a simple hydrogen atom
                      turned on its head, for the first time
                      trapped in a magnetic mesh.

scattering skin,
bone, muscle, gouts
of blood, the stuff that makes me.

                      No cataclysmic rendezvous,
                      instead, a provocative laser
                      begs for a quantum leap.

From bedroom to kitchen,
from home to school to work
to school to shops to home,

                One positron flashes between
                shells, stealing photons
                from the ultra-violet,

I check cupboards, fridge,
google a new recipe
start frying onion and garlic,

                you measure what's gone –
                two lines on the spectrum.
                Time to start writing

chop carrots, what the hell
is quinoa? Our youngest
brawls with homework.

                the paper. Nature
                should take it, Nobel Prize
                to follow. You battle

I sweep the floor, try
to reconstruct myself,
drink a third glass of wine.

                with passive voice, eventually
                come home to burnt dinner.
                What the hell is quinoa?

Quantum dating

You'll never find a quark at a singles bar. They prefer to spin in threes, each dressed in a different colour.

An unstable quark might pair up with an antiquark. Such couplings never last long. With luck, you may catch a quark on the rebound.

Keep a count of the W-bosons in your vicinity. Quarks are notorious for hooking up with them on a whim, and dumping them just as thoughtlessly. They don't mean anything by it, but it does change their flavour.

Ignore the rumours of tetraquarks and pentaquarks. Involvement with these exotic hadrons is only for the adventurous, and is strongly discouraged.

When you've got your quark, find out if it is up, down, strange, charm, top, or bottom. It doesn't matter to them, they're not fussy, but you shouldn't confuse your charmed bottom with your double bottom. No-one knows what that might lead to.

Blackboard

I brush chalk from my hands.
I've finished.

The boy sneezes.
He puts his Nintendo down,
mutters: does that really mean anything?
I say: wipe your nose.

How do I tell a small, scowling child
that this final set of chalk marks,
this glorious, transcendent equation,
unifies the four fundamental forces?
How do I tell him that I have calculated
the true nature of gravity?

I say: yes. It explains everything.
It tells me why you are here,
where you came from, how our world
and all the other worlds began,
and how they will end.

He says: bet it can't tell me
what I'm having for tea tonight.
I say: beans on toast.
He says: and ice-cream for pudding?

I study the chalk marks.
I say: yes, and ice-cream for pudding.

A proton as a serving of minestrone

Rules for eating soup

You have no time at all
to eat the whole lot.
There is no bread.
You can only eat one slice of carrot
with one piece of onion,
or a pea with a chunk of potato.
You must take precisely
the same amount of broth
with each mouthful.

The broth

This holds the vegetables
keeping them together.
Its consistency
constantly changes
but there is always exactly
the right volume.

Leftovers

Although you'll never
know how many
of each vegetable
or how much broth
your serving contains,
and those numbers change
from moment to moment,
there will always be
two carrots, one pea
and three teaspoons
of broth left over

once you've consumed
an uncountable number
of mouthfuls. That
defines minestrone.

Notes:

1. protons are subatomic particles contained in the nucleus of atoms
2. vegetables correspond to quarks
3. broth corresponds to gluons
4. many other types of soup are available

Waltz

I have a
    leg full of
        bites – this one
            how do they
                know to bite
                    only this
              leg? It's the
          leg the cat
            snuggles so
                less far to
                    travel the
                        searching for
                  uncomplex
              answers leaves
          me in a
        pirouette
          so deep in-
            side me my
              atoms my
                protons my
                    neutrons el-
                      ectrons in-
                        side them ex-
                    otic beasts
                  shimmy ap-
                pearing and

                pairing and
             parting ap-
         pearing and
       pairing and
     parting ap-
pearing and
     pairing and
       parting and
         one two three
            one two three
              one two three
           steps are ob-
         scure I just
     follow and
        don't ask those
           questions ex-
             otics con-
               tinue their
                 dance and the
                   fleas keep on
                     biting...

Rebirth as a quantum mechanic

1. Touch

Trace a line along your arm. Shiver. Fine hairs rise up, pulling at your skin. The senses of finger touching arm and arm touched by finger cannot be separated. Yet the two have never made contact, cannot make contact. You can never touch anything. Until you redefine the word *touch*.

2. Wave/particle duality

Is light a wave or a particle?
                    [This is the wrong question
                          The right question is   [*What is light?*]

3. Curiosity

How could you not yearn to wrap your mind around a world where particles are smaller than the smallest they can be, and nothing behaves the way you *know* it should? How could your questions not flood into the vast spaces between the nucleus of every atom and its electron shells?

4. Electrons

                    [Words pull out wrong notions...

Electrons spin.
                    [They *behave* as if they spin
                          but they don't   they can't]

Electrons are particles.
                            [They are   wavefunctions
                            defining where you *might*
                            find them]

Electrons jump from shell to shell.
                            [This leap does not   ever
                            pass through the in between]]

5. The Electromagnetic Interaction

...rest your head on my shoulder
      ...wrap both arms around me
      ...breathe a kiss on my lips
...it stops just short of touching
      ...the electrons of your molecules
      ...repel the electrons of mine
...inside atoms, between molecules
      ...the weight of the air on your skin

6. Now

As you breathe, question the air,
How do you   [empty space made up of more empty space]
push my lungs outwards?

If you see a cat in a box, wonder,
How does light   [something that cannot be imagined]
project you into my mind?

When you embrace your children, ask,
How can we feel   [when we can never touch]
each other's warmth?

Counting virtual particles

1.

I always count my footsteps, it makes
the walking go quicker. Trees growing

through railings take time to wrap new
wood around angles of rusting steel.

I count cars too, using that old trick to count
to ninety-nine without using toes. My toes

are busy walking. The cars don't know
they're being counted. Through the path

between burberis bushes, and the trees
keep growing while my fingers count.

Cars flicker into sight between leaves
and rough thorns, cancel out my footsteps

which keep their beat. The leaves say it's autumn,
the sun hasn't followed. My feet count

the path towards winter as trees gather
themselves inward. Railings don't care

about seasons, my feet and my fingers don't
feel the sun or the growing of the trees,

they just keep counting steady footsteps
and quickly disappearing cars.

2.

Beyond my senses, I know counted cars still travel.
Like images of a car between tree branches,

my footsteps, once counted, are gone;
their force exhausted in the space between here

and there. This dance between non-being and being
takes place too in the atoms of my feet

and my fingers and the cars and the trees
as gluons flicker to hold in place

the core of each atom's nucleus,
flashing through existence.

No fingers can count these particles,
we can only know the residual force

which binds protons and neutrons,
the force which remains constant,

itself carried by inconstant mesons
emerging briefly from the gluons' dance.

My plodding footsteps take me forward
as particles within my feet are born

and die in their uncountable millions
to ensure my feet remain the same.

Randomness

                                          an oak leaf
                                        fallen on a mole hill

                              covering some number
                              of ants and woodlice

        a defined structure
        of decaying cells

                atoms waiting
                for other structures

                          the decay of one
                          radioactive particle

    trapped in a box
    with a cat

                              which must be
                              neither alive or dead

          must be
          both alive and dead

                        a heart-shaped pebble
                        swept by a wave

       solid as a rock
       yet inside steady particles

ever-changing sets
of even smaller particles

                the sea swells
                to a broken metronome

                              the frequency
                              of raindrops

                            how hard they hit
                            how far they splash

                                the way H_2O molecules
                                slide over each other

whether my umbrella
will blow away

                  a dead field mouse
                  by my back door

    if it had foraged
    in another garden tonight

                would probably be
                breathing still

Line indents from: www.random.org

White dwarf (a day by the sea)

Five billion years from now, our sun will have finished.
It will collapse into a super-dense ball
of nuclear matter, sharing the leftovers
with an electron sea. Gravity will crush
holidaymakers together until waves engulf all,
devouring their space.

On a crowded beach we set up our windbreak,
catch the sun, settle into the summer together,

slap on the Ambre Solaire. Adults collapse, children dive
to the bottom of the sea. I am young, invincible,

it doesn't matter that the sandstone making up the cliffs
reaches for space, land slips uncertainly.

We climb into the sunshine until
the foreshadowed lunchtime collapse

onto the tartan blanket, blistering together. My brother and I
fetch lunch, Dad says sand in sandwiches doesn't matter.

Mum's smile crunches, collapses. The afternoon
brings ice-cream, the sun burns fuel ferociously,

pushing us into the sea. We squeeze lips and eyelids
tight together, sink to where crabs escape the sun.

On this beach, the gaps between grains of sand
are ours until the tide comes in and the castle is lost.

What do we care about solar collapse? We have our beach,
our waves, our sea filling our late evening space

while we soak up the sunset together
and crunching sand no longer matters. We're a family

coloured red by the sun. I learned to swim
in that sea, no matter what came after,

we were together in that space
where the sun, at the far horizon, collapsed.

The strong interaction
for RLP

We make our home
in our thoughts
shaping walls

into bookcases
for our books.
I see everything

in your eyes.
I need nothing
more than

the way I need
this soft rain
falling on our roof

gently urging us
to open the
bright windows.

You will find me
snug in a nook
behind your eyes

looking through
those windows
at the soft rain

and bookcases
filled with books
our old friends.

Collisions

She's worked out a way to destroy a planet by building a solar-system-sized hadron collider. She admits it's not possible, yet. She cried for days when Tinkerbell died, the cat she'd only met twice, the cat who would run the twenty-three-mile circuit of the large hadron collider to avoid her. She mobilises armies online and promises me Lundy when she rules the world. She stuffs her mind full of ideas and propels them towards each other to see what happens. Then she stays awake all night writing the results into steampunk collisions. I hope the electromagnetic force that her skull is made from will contain the explosion when it comes, but I cannot guarantee your safety in this likely eventuality. I think she cries at night sometimes, the crashing of her tears is how her bed was broken. I think she is a god made mortal, I think that is why the cat ran scared. Her skin stretches over bone, there is no fat, she barely eats. Perhaps she is death, perhaps she will truly end us all.

Decay
i.m. RCH

Rusting in the corner of our yard, a shovel
hangs from a nail.

It has dug ditches in its day,
furrowed the soil for crops,
hollowed graves in the living earth,

raised blisters on generations of hands.

Its blade is dull now, its handle
splintering around crumbled rivets.

My father used this shovel to excavate
the roots of the dead sycamore
which shattered the walls of our home.

Today it is my father who is diseased,
too weak to threaten anything.

But still he brandishes
the ghost of this shovel in death's face
swears he will take that scythe
and smash it.

Not long now until I must take another shovel,
raise my own crop of blisters,
digging where once a sycamore grew.

Jubilate Astra et Hominem
After Christopher Smart

For the stars themselves are vast and empty
For they are made in space and by space and of space
For their self-immolation persists to time and nothingness
For their songs are silent and still they deafen you
For you are vast and empty too, though your deeds be mighty
For your being comes from sparks given off by empty stars
For the atoms within you are no more than flecks in the void
For you can never touch another person save through words
For the words from your mouth are only broken air
For your stories echo the song of the stars
For you know that song must exist
For it could not be otherwise
For that song is an elegy as long as the time before time began
For your time is short
For in that time we will resound upon the edges of the universe
For in that time we will touch a thousand thousand men
For in that time we will be alone in your own vast emptiness
For after that time our bones will crumble within the earth
For our flesh will rot and maggots will choke your tongue
For the stars will never know our passing
For they have no time, for they have too much time
For we can never know the size of the vastness
For we can never know the depth of the emptiness
For our time is short
For my speed is governed by the stars
For their song pulls them onward
For I must follow, or crumble and rot
For their sparks are burning brightly within me
For as much as they pull me, I too pull them
For strength does not live in size or depth
For tonight I will walk on fire
For the laws of the universe state I will not be burned
For I can defeat the heat of the elements
For I can sing louder through air that is broken
For my song shall reach the stars
For my time is short

GLOSSARY

Antimatter: a collision between any particle and its anti-particle leads to their mutual annihilation.

Boson: the elementary bosons are force carriers that function as the 'glue' holding matter together.

Cat in a box: a thought experiment devised by Erwin Schrödinger in which a cat, a flask of poison, and a radioactive source are placed in a sealed box to illustrate the fallacy that a particle can exist in all states at once until observed.

Dark matter: a hypothetical form of matter that is thought to account for approximately 85% of the matter in the universe.

Electromagnetic force: one of the four fundamental forces.

Electron: a subatomic particle which orbits the nucleus of an atom.

Fundamental forces: there are four fundamental forces – electromagnetic force, weak and strong nuclear forces, and gravitational force.

Gluon: an elementary particle that 'glues' quarks together to form other particles such as protons and neutrons.

Lepton: an elementary particle that does not undergo strong interactions.

Meson: an unstable subatomic particle.

Neutron: a subatomic particle that forms part of the nucleus of an atom.

Positron: the antimatter partner of the electron.

Proton: a subatomic particle that forms part of the nucleus of an atom.

Quantum mechanics: a branch of physics which explains the behaviour of matter on the scale of atoms and subatomic particles.

Quark: an elementary particle and a fundamental constituent of matter.

The strong interaction: one of the four known fundamental interactions. It holds most ordinary matter together.

Virtual particle: a transient fluctuation that exhibits some characteristics of an ordinary particle. The longer a virtual particle exists the closer its characteristics come to that of the ordinary particle.

White dwarf: a small star remnant that is very dense and faint.

ELIZABETH HOURSTON

Contents

The road to Hermaness	67
After the skreever	68
Brodgar	69
At the Standing Stones of Stenness	70
Maeshowe	71
Song of clay vessels	72
Sunrise, Orkney	73
Two love stories	74
The curlew	75
To the fiddler	76
Lost at sea	77
The lifeboatman and his wife	78
Beachcomber	79
Kitchener's Memorial, Marwick Head, Orkney	80
Between weathers	81
Runes, Maeshowe	82
Waystop	84
Maithes	85
Portrait of a twenty-first century Viking	86
Grandmother	87
Dreamcatcher	88
Chiaroscuro	89
Mists over Malham	90
Midnight	92
Finally	93
Glossary	94

The road to Hermaness

Do you know the road to Hermaness

where the land meets the sea
and the sea meets the sky

where the wind sucks the breath
out of you and scours your bones

where salt reddens your eyeballs
and stings bitter on your tongue?

Leave behind the houses and fields
the man-made dykes and follow

the unmarked track until you come
to the wild sea and raging sky

where dishevelled feathers flutter
and ravening bonxies dive

where the light is white and hard
and the colours true.

After the skreever

white horses come galloping in from the deep,
snorting secrets dredged from the darkest
places where roiling waters surge
in green-veined whirlpools, where

beyond the eddying swelkies,
pink-tipped corals grow through
skaad-men's heads, and monsters
and strange creatures dwell.

Listen. Catch that wild uncanny roar
rumbling in from eldritch depths.
Stand by the shore and listen
for it is fleeting, blown on spindrifted air.

Brodgar

i
the sky grey
a low bowl of hills
the lochs like beaten steel

and
the stones
rooted
in the earth

ii
beyond Hoy
the lifeblood of the day
seeps away

the lode star
rises
in the east

iii
in the fullness of the year
and in its dregs
solstice suns
shaft
the chambered tomb

earth
trembles

a small wind
ruffles the grasses

and
a teeack cries

At the Standing Stones of Stenness

Dwarfed,
they stood here too

among heather thatched
with cocks and hens, tormentil
and the purple fleck of vetch,

the air heady with clover
and the sharp tang of meadowsweet,

the bees busy.

Teeacks stagger anxious across the sky

this way

                  this way

                                  a false trail

and the stones silent.

Maeshowe

Crawl to the dark centre

where the stone
is slabbed
perfectly;

feel it cold
and smooth
beneath your fingers.

Crawl to the dark centre

where they crept
to worship
their gods

or bury their dead
or carve their lusts:
Ingigerth, loveliest of women.

Crawl to the dark centre

where a man
lost
his wits,

where, in an empty vault,
you know no more
than they.

Song of clay vessels

Arcing grey wastes of sea
a gull cried *cullya*.
Old Bruga shaped the pot
between his hands
and smiled.
Its symmetry was satisfactory
and its full round belly pleasing to the eye.

◊◊◊◊◊◊◊◊◊◊◊◊◊◊◊◊◊◊◊◊◊◊◊◊◊◊◊◊◊◊◊◊◊◊

Archaeologically speaking, a masterpiece,
the perfect specimen, she says,
running her caked finger
round the sand clay rim.
While overhead
a gull cries *cullya*
across a restlessness of ocean.

Sunrise, Orkney

air

    still as held breath

        land

            blue on a low horizon

sea

    a glamsy of honey

        red-ware   duck-egg   green

    sliced by an oyster catcher's cry

light

    bends

        wind

            chabbles

                patterns

                    shift

there...   now...   there...   again...

    the watchers pass

sea

    a shimmer of honey

        red-ware   duck-egg   grey

land

    dark on a low horizon

        still as held breath

    air

Two love stories

The bones lie
in a shallow grave,
muddied and yellow.

My God!

Grasses stir
on the dig's edge.

His fingers tighten
till he can feel her bone
beneath his own.

He thinks of soft
flesh, loose dark hair,
urgent breath.

One male, five feet ten.
One female, five feet three.
Artefacts: brooch, pin, comb.

Date: early eighth century.

A curlew keens
from the whispering sedge.

Grasses stir.

The curlew

On the first evening I hear again
that melancholy rising call,
piercing the dew-damp summer dusk,
haunting the shore with memories.

I listen: *huilpe   huilpe.*
Wild poetry scores the sky,
the sorrowful lovelorn song
of the archer of the rising moon.

To the fiddler

Under the cold furrow
you discover the root
and unfurl the seed,

fires at the centre;
you unravel the rainbow
and encircle the stars;

you plumb unsounded seas
and swim with selkies
in caves of ice.

And I would have you,
maker of music;

I would have you,
dreamer of dreams

if you could show me
one silver penny.

It is Sigurd, who holds steady
through rain and storm,
who will sow my seed.

But, when the music skirls
for the whirling dance,
I will remember you.

I will remember how
your furrow sparkled
with the hoofprints of stars.

Lost at sea

The moon bleaches
whitewashed houses
by the harbour wall.

She turns and murmurs
in her dream.

He sets his sail
by the Fair Isle
and casts his net.

Drifts of silver
flash his mesh.

Round the Ness
a drunken crew
roust, loudmouthed.

Timbers crash;
a startled seagull cries.

In the suck of the tide
cold currents
tongue the drowned

and pick dreams
bare.

The lifeboatman and his wife

He
sea heaves
sky dives
looming crests
swallow the moon

from the waves'
trough
hissing foam is
heaven high

and hell judders
at his feet

        She
        wound tight
        in cold sheets
        not listening
        to the wind's
        cracking

        not breathing
        for fear
        one tremor more
        might tip the
        balance
        of the gale

                They
                in the dawn
                a welcoming
                of arms

                and two
                half-told
                tales

Beachcomber

Returned from a life at sea,
he worked a croft above the banks,
salt sour. Under the cliff
he watched the flotsam of the firth
swirl in on the whorling tide.

Driftwood, rope, boots, brushes
without bristles, rotten fruit,
leaves, even one time a mine
washed in from the war.

He prodded clumped weed,
teetered on slippery rocks
to capture spars of wood,
piled his treasures above
the high tide mark.

Waves pounding the geo
brought memories of seafaring days,
of Arctic ice floes creaking as they calved,
of sultry nights in Rio with his mates.

Here, a poor summer, gales,
lashing rain, crops flattened,
a beast gone before the shore…
The last glimmerings of a winter sun
stained The Knab red. The sea,

his old unfailing friend, caressed his feet.
In the thin cold light of dawn, tangled
with the weed and wreckage of a flowing tide,
his body washed up on the deserted bay.

Kitchener's Memorial, Marwick Head, Orkney

Easter morning. Larksong bubbling
and teeack eggs tucked neatly at our feet.
The rumble of Atlantic breakers
lathering the rocks with salt-frothed air.
We lift our faces to the sun.

As we near the Head,
the stench of seabirds
catches in our throats

and the Memorial
                       glooms.

Exploding seas mine our darkening minds:
the tug of under-tow, the skreever's shriek,
the choke of rain, mouths gaping... gulping...
and the rock face slippery
and sheer.

We pause.

                       The morning quivers.

Then the rise is crested.
Hoy lies before us
and the hills of Scotland,
blue and clear.

Between weathers

We are at sea.

            Astern, cloud and mist
lour low on Thurso Bay.

            Sudden sun
scorches the cliffs of Hoy to embered red.

A sough of wind, fickle as history,
funnels through Rackwick and falls still.
Ahead, the Kame is lost in fretted haar.

A yellowed gannet hangs beside the Hamnavoe,
poised

            and I turn again to you.

Runes, Maeshowe

Jerusalem farers, we did not think to spend the night
tomb enclosed so near our Jarl's feasting hall,
where the ox roasts dripping on the spit
and the deep brewed ale flows free;
where golden maidens, tresses braided to the waist,
strew sweet smelling rushes in expectant chambers,
young, supple as saplings and warm with the glow of life.

Here is a cold homecoming,
grey stone hewn for death
clammy under our fingers,
white bones rattling loose.
We did not brave Jerusalem for this.

When I think of that city – a jewel in the desert –
and the knights of Europe, heavy in harness,
cumbersome on the burning sand, champions
of courtly love in a land of savagery...

Tempered in the icy forges of the north,
we knew better how to handle
the infidel Saracen.

We captured a tyrant's castle in Galicia,
fought the heathen Moor in Spain
and took a dromond in the Middle Sea.

We bathed in Jordan and were
received in Istanbul, courted
by Menelaus for his Varangian guard.
But, thank God, we escaped that fate
and sailed for Italy.

When I think of Narbonne –
its soft, sweet delights
and the seductive charms
of amorous Ermingarde –
Maeshowe is no welcome after such things.

But even here, entombed in darkness,
we have left our mark, riding out the storm
with idle whittling: lion of the Ringerike,
carved by Bjorn; runes cut deep
by the axe of Gauk Trandilson;
verses for Ingibjorg, fair widow.

When at last we make safe haven,
the songs of the Icelandic skalds
will ring around the feasting halls
from here to Greenland and beyond.

A cold homecoming it would be indeed
were these poor scratchings our only epitaph.

Waystop
12th century: St Magnus' bones are carried from Birsay to Kirkwall

Those poor bones

jiggle in their box,
rattle like a bairn's toy.

The men, footsore and weary,
wipe the sweat from their brows
and the dust from their eyes,

quaff the proferred ale
in great, gusty gulps,
exhale in long sighs

like the wind sooching
on a winter's night.

Those poor, bare bones.

We countryfolk gawp, think
of songs Magnus sang in the midst of battle,
of death dealt by the kiss of the axe,
of miracles wrought on Birsay shore

and we cross ourselves and
kneel down on the unyielding earth.

Maithes

He knew the landmarks of the bay
like his own hand, a listing of lifelines.
To the north west the Brough,
last landfall before America;
to the south the cliffs of Marwick Head,
where Kitchener lost his life.
Line up the headlands of Gorie's Bite
to steer by the deep channel Yimma-Yamma
and run straight across the bay, to ground
the keel on the shingle at Castra Geo
below the Point of Buckquoy.

When the roofs of Grew pitched into sight
over the cliffs at Garson, he knew
the shoals of cuithes and lythe lay ready
to take the lines and gasp their lives out
on the bloodied thwart, eyes
glazing in the failing light.

On days he could not raise a crew,
he made his way with caisie, wand
and line along the shore to Shua Geo,
the Flags, or Choin or, depending
on the wind and tide, to the north side
of the bay to Doonaminya,
Clett or Skipigeo. There he prised
limpets free, mashed them to a pulp
and cast them in the sea as bait.
Basket full, in the glimmerings,
he made his way by Gillie's land
and St Magnus' kirk to home.

Portrait of a twenty-first century Viking
In memory of a Shetland uncle

He stood in the doorway,
thumbs in his braces,
knees bent forward,
torso leaning back,
balanced it seemed
in impossible equilibrium.

Rognvald Kolsson ran in there,
he said, nodding his head towards the voe,
and speaking as if it were only
yesterday.

Driven in before a south east gale.
Bloody foolishness. It's a
wonder they survived at all.

Standing there with his hair
blowing in the wind, and his grey
beard thick about his face,
he might have been on that boat himself,
those blue eyes
straight from Bergen
and the year 1148.

Grandmother

Half smiling, she squints into the sun,
looks straight at me, unseeing.
I stare back at her, devour
the droop of her eyelids, her nose, the lines
around her mouth and eyes that show
how she has laughed and cried.

I see her hair, parted in the middle,
drawn softly back behind her neck;
study her hands, loose by her side,
fingering her skirt. I see the door
behind her partly open, flowers
sprouting by the wall.

I grieve for her because she never
knew her son would take a wife;
never knew that wife would bear
a child who would peer at the photo
of someone she never knew,
searching for a likeness.

Dreamcatcher

By the light of the moon
she picked the willow,
fashioned it to a circle.

By the light of the sun
she stripped the nettles,
dyed them earth-red.

By the light of the stars
she wove the strands,
mimicking the spider.

By the flames of the fire
she threaded the feathers,
strung the beads.

By the half-light of dusk
she hung the catcher
by the head of the cradle.

By the guttering candle
she watched the nightmares
snag in the web.

By the glow of the lamp
she watched sweet dreams
slide down the feathers

into your life.

Chiaroscuro

In the shadowed kitchen a young boy
and his mother sit shelling peas.
The door is open and the garden
filled with sunshine. A blackbird
sings. A warm wind lifts the fronds
of the wisteria. *One day you will follow
the wind*, she says. *You will choose
your way and leave.*
        Silent
he thumbs the peas from the pod,
firm and green, into the glazed bowl.
He shakes his head.
        Never.

The light changes. Across the room
there falls a sudden chill.

Mists over Malham
For a friend who has Alzheimer's disease

Like fingers clinging to a lost life,
dry-stone walls clutch the land,
enclosing emptiness.

Mist mizzles.

We tramp the rough path.

Below, the river churns;
a lone heron stands.

You stop to consider
the light on a golden leaf,
the shape of a petal,

a shaft of sunshine
on the rooftops below.

Hands encourage.

Come

 We tramp the path

            across the contours of the fells

                the wetness of grass

                    the harsh limestone.

You consider the rough texture of bark
the startling greenness of moss.

Cloud thickens.
                Rain settles
                              on hair, faces, eyelashes.

Boots grow heavy.

We climb towards
        the limestone outcrops
                the bewildering wasteland.

    This way…
               hold my hand.

Mists swirl.

Midnight

to be there
on a night like this

stars glister from a sky
deeper than oceans

ice crisps each blade
of grass   silence hangs

on such a night

a blue hare crouches
in frosted bracken

eyes dark as peat pools
the merest shiver

to be there
breathless

Finally

at the edge now
I look across the water
a fine haar hovers
whiting the horizon

waves lap my feet

behind me lie uncharted
folds of land
and the pathways
I have chosen

people come and go

a fret fidgets in from the sea
creeps over the sands
floods the valleys
obscures the mountain tops

all that is familiar dims

voices become a whisper
fade... fade...

waves lap the shore

GLOSSARY

bonxie	great skua
caisie	basket
chabbles	ruffles
cocks and hens	bird's foot trefoil
cuithes	coalfish
cullya	call of a gull
dyke	dry stone wall
fret	sea mist
geo	narrow bay
glamsy	shimmer
haar	sea mist
lythe	pollack
maithes	marks to guide a boat from the sea
red-ware	red seaweed
skaad man's head	sea urchin
skreever	strong gale; hurricane
swelkies	whirlpools
teeack	lapwing
voe	small bay
wand	simple fishing rod